THIS WALKER BOOK BELONGS TO:

This book is dedicated to
Emily and Felix and all the other
children who discover that reading
is fun once you know how to do it.
S.H.

For my long-suffering husband, Ian, with love.
M.M.C.

Educational Consultant

Prue Goodwin
Reading and Language Information Centre
The University of Reading

First published 1998 by Walker Books Ltd
87 Vauxhall Walk, London SE11 5HJ

This edition published 1999

10 9 8 7 6 5 4 3 2

Text © 1998 Sarah Hayes
Illustrations © 1998 Margaret Chamberlain

Printed in Hong Kong

British Library Cataloguing in Publication Data
A catalogue record for this book is
available from the British Library.

ISBN 0-7445-6936-2

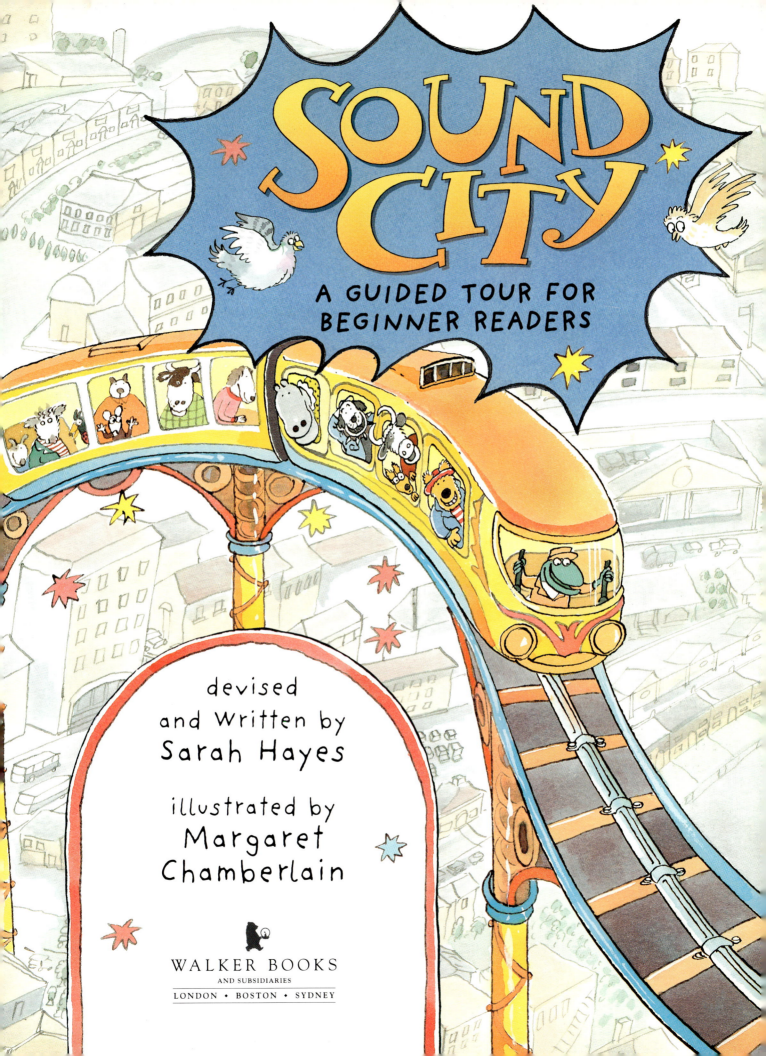

SOUND CITY

A GUIDED TOUR FOR BEGINNER READERS

devised
and Written by
Sarah Hayes

illustrated by
Margaret
Chamberlain

WALKER BOOKS
AND SUBSIDIARIES
LONDON · BOSTON · SYDNEY

CONTENTS

ABOUT

SOUND CITY helps new readers to *hear* the sounds of letters, and the sounds of words. It shows them how to *recognize* the words those letters and sounds make and, most important of all – to *understand* what the words mean. That's all part of learning to read.

Exploring **SOUND CITY** encourages new readers to find the patterns in words, especially words that rhyme. Catchy verses like *Fred's Bread* or *Rough Stuff* show how different letter combinations can make similar sounds.

SOUND CITY helps new readers to discover for themselves that sounds, put together, make words – words they can read.

HOW TO USE THIS BOOK

SOUND CITY is meant for sharing. Adults and children can explore the city together by talking about what's going on in the pictures and saying sounds and words out loud. Guessing at sounds and trying to sound-out words are part of reading too.

The first two pages, *Alpha Betty's Junk Shop*, show the alphabet sounds and the letter combinations (or blends) used to begin words. Listening for beginning letters is one of the first steps in recognizing sounds.

Each double page that follows explores a different sound or group of sounds. Look for the blue letters in the title – they're the key sounds you'll find in the pictures. Similar sounds are grouped together so a new reader gets to know and expect them.

THIS BOOK

HOW TO EXPLORE SOUND CITY

There's no fixed sequence to the pages in **SOUND CITY**, so you can let your reader choose any picture to explore. Each page has lots to look at and talk about, so you'll need time to take in all the details. And you can look back, jump ahead or return and re-read any time you want to.

THINGS TO DO ON EACH PAGE

① Look at the picture to see what's going on and which part of the city you're in.

② Look at the blue letters in the title – they're the key sounds on the page.

③ Read the verse aloud a couple of times. Your child may want to read some words or lines with you.

④ Point to a few words with the key sound in them. You and your reader may find different ways of spelling the key sounds.

⑤ Solve Private Eye's puzzle.

Each time you read together, your child may find more words that use the key sounds. Listening to the sounds, looking for words that contain them, saying the words aloud and understanding them – that's reading!

THE SIGNS IN SOUND CITY

Like any real city, **SOUND CITY** is full of sounds, signs and activity. Here are some of the symbols you'll find:

- Titles look like this (key sounds in blue) ▶ *MISS LIZZY*

- Arrows like this are labels for things ▶ ink

- Action words are shown like this ▶ skip skip

- Speech bubbles look like this ▶ That's silly.

I am Private Eye.

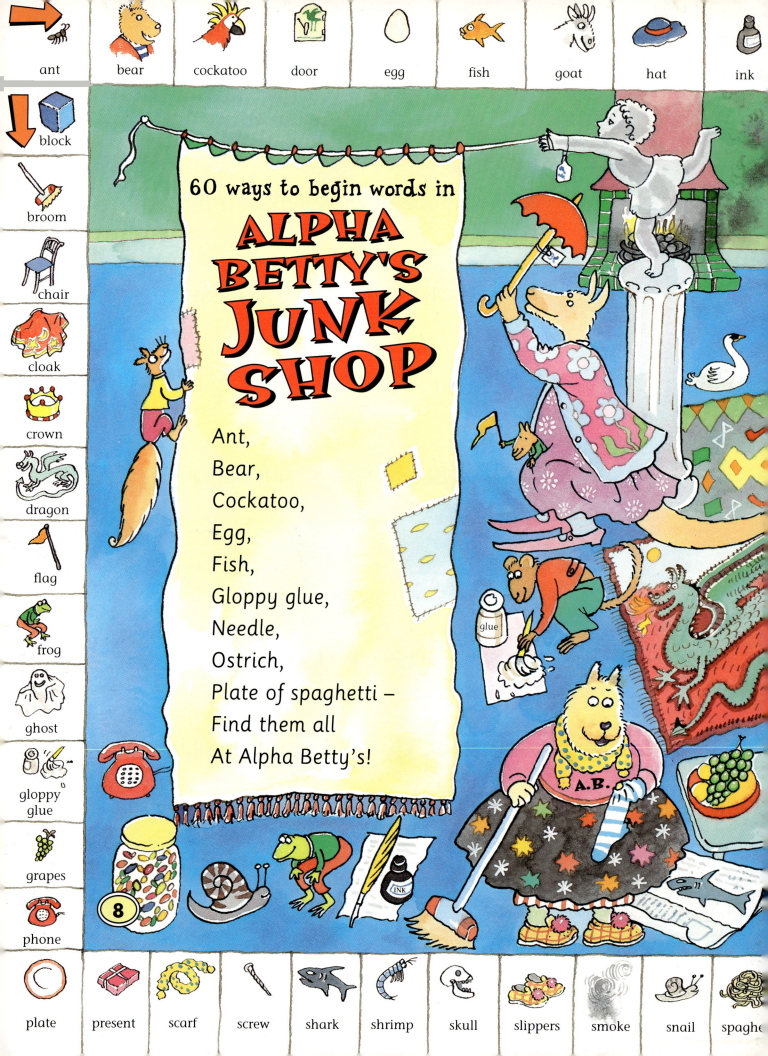

ant
bear
cockatoo
door
egg
fish
goat
hat
ink

block
broom
chair
cloak
crown
dragon
flag
frog
ghost
gloppy glue
grapes
phone

60 ways to begin words in

ALPHA BETTY'S JUNK SHOP

Ant,
Bear,
Cockatoo,
Egg,
Fish,
Gloppy glue,
Needle,
Ostrich,
Plate of spaghetti —
Find them all
At Alpha Betty's!

8

plate
present
scarf
screw
shark
shrimp
skull
slippers
smoke
snail
spaghe

lly beans
kangaroo
lamp
mouse
needle
ostrich
pie
quill-pen
rat
sock
table
umbrella
violin
watch
xylophone
yo-yo
zebra
20
All 60 labelled objects are hidden in Alpha Betty's shop. Can you find them?
9
splash
spring
squirrel
statue
string
swan
thread
thumb
trumpet
20
twenty
wheel

FAT CAT

Drat!

SPLAT!

A fat cat-cat
Had a rat-rat-rat,
And the rat-rat-rat
Got sat on.
"What a flat rat-rat,"
Said the fat cat-cat,
And then she put
Her hat on.

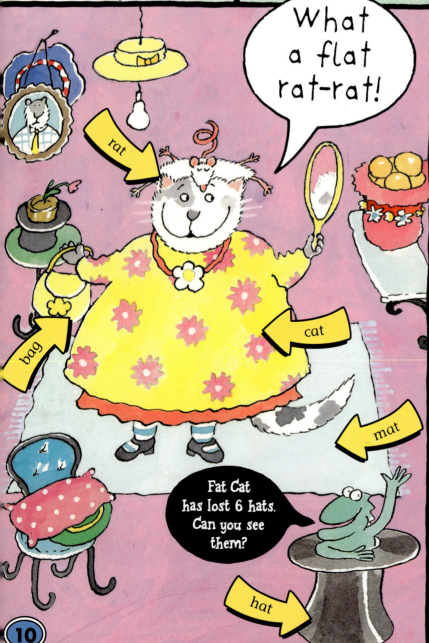

What a flat rat-rat!

rat

bag

cat

mat

hat

Fat Cat has lost 6 hats. Can you see them?

Ed

Ned

Ted

FRED'S BREAD

Fred

Heather

Ed said to Ned,
And Ned said to Ted,
And Ted said to Fred,
"This bread is red!"
Fred said to Ted,
"It's not just red,
It's heavy as lead."
"Must be the weather,"
Said Heather,
And she made the bread
Instead.
"Light as a feather!"
Said Heather.
Ed, Ned and Ted
Buried the red bread.
Fred went to bed
Instead.

MISS LIZZY

Miss Lizzy's
In a tizzy
When her kids
Are busy busy
Doing things
Miss Lizzy's kids
Must never do!

TOP DOG'S COFFEE

I want coffee
In a pot, pot, pot.
I want coffee
That is hot, hot, hot.
I want coffee
To be—
STOP! STOP! STOP!
I got coffee
With a wasp on top!

❶ Spotty Dog got Top Dog's coffee.

clock

TOP DOG'S OFFICE

knock knock

coffee po[t]

❹ Top Dog dropped the coffee pot.

SPLOSH

❼ Top Dog coughed.

cough cough

Spotty Dog!!! What's this? A wasp in my coffee.

❽ Top Dog got cross ...

Drop dead, Top Dog! This job's not what I want. I'm off!

I am cross!

watch

but Spotty Dog got a lot crosser.

14

CHUCK'S TRUCK

A dove
And a duck
Sat under
A truck,
But the dove
Got lovey-dovey.
"Yuck!"
Said the duck.
"Yuck! Yuck!"
Said the duck,
And gave the dove
A shove-y!

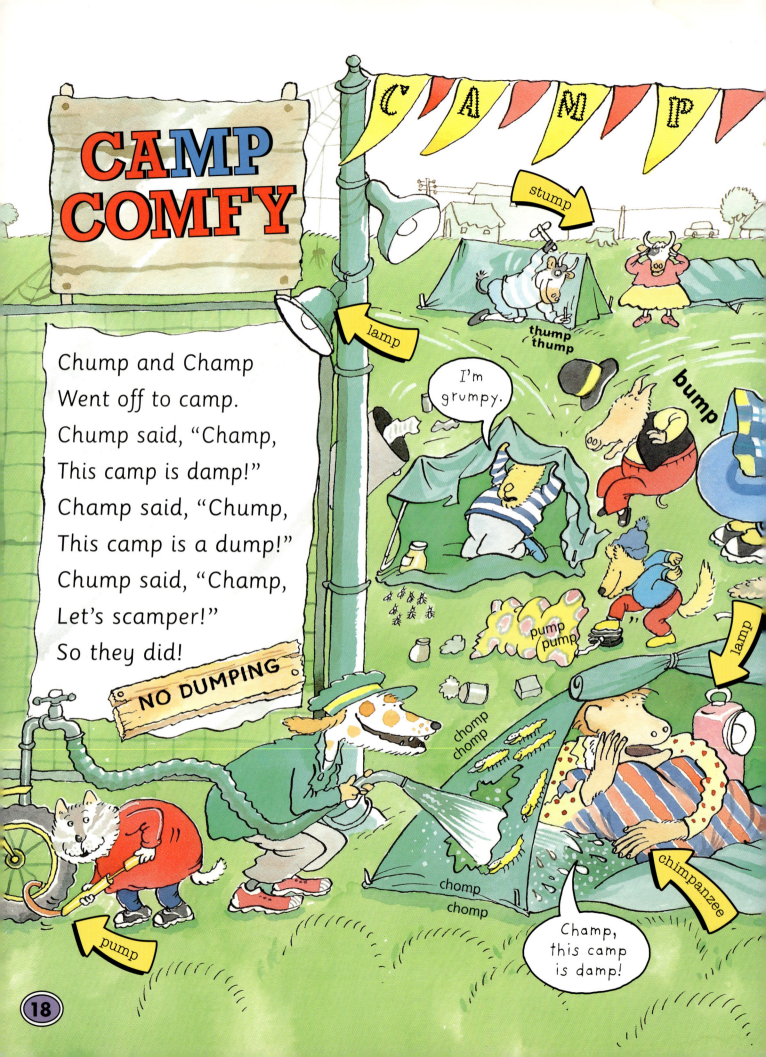

CAMP COMFY

Chump and Champ
Went off to camp.
Chump said, "Champ,
This camp is damp!"
Champ said, "Chump,
This camp is a dump!"
Chump said, "Champ,
Let's scamper!"
So they did!

18

CHANCE TO DANCE

Lance danced
Whenever
He got the chance.
He danced
On fences,
He danced
On benches,
He danced
On branches,
He danced
In trenches.
The only place
That Lance
Never danced
Was Nancy's
Non-Stop
Dancing Dome!

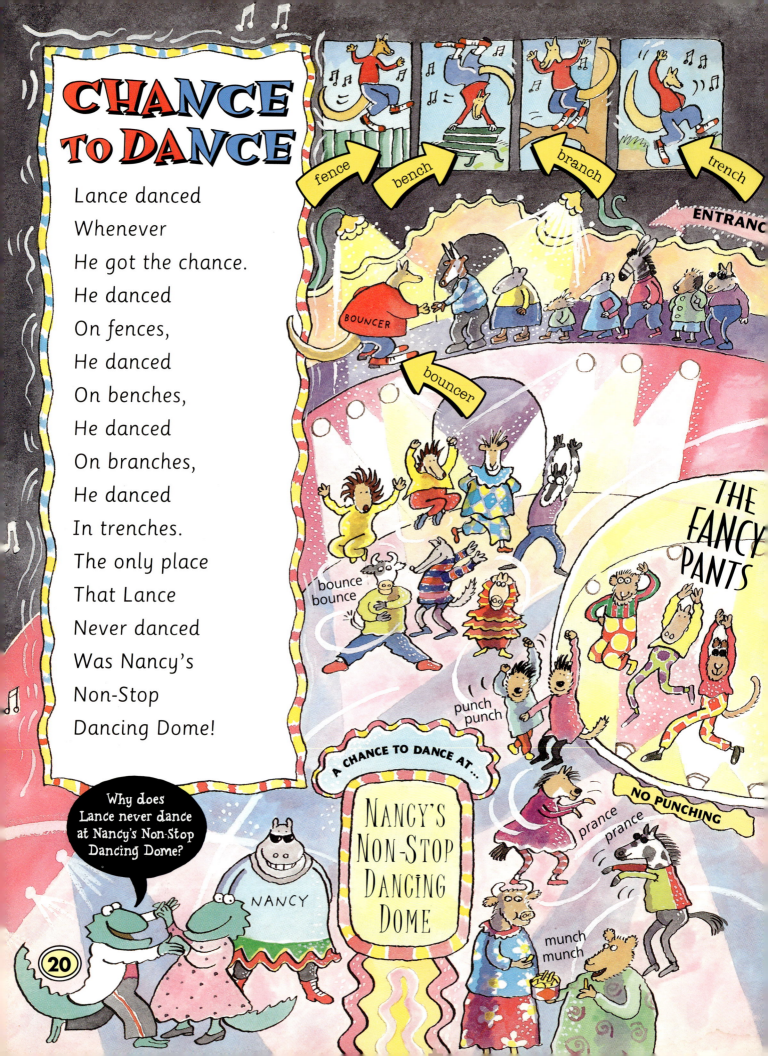

fence

bench

branch

trench

ENTRANCE

BOUNCER

bouncer

THE FANCY PANTS

bounce bounce

punch punch

A CHANCE TO DANCE AT...

NO PUNCHING

prance prance

Why does Lance never dance at Nancy's Non-Stop Dancing Dome?

NANCY

NANCY'S NON-STOP DANCING DOME

munch munch

20

CAN'T FIND GRANDPA

Can't find Grandpa
And I don't know
Where he went.
He isn't in the fountain
And he isn't in the tent.
He isn't in the duck pond,
He isn't in the sand –
Is he at the band stand
Standing by the band?

21

JINGLE-JANGLE JUGGLING

Who can
Sing a song
And swing along?
Who can
Swing along
And bang a gong?
Who can
Bang a gong
And jingle-jangle
Bangles?
Who can
Jingle-jangle bangles
And juggle triangles?
Who can?
The only
Singing
Swinging
Banging
Jingle-jangle-juggling
Orang-u-tan!

Dad's got the plunger,
Mum's got the sponge,
Who filled the sink
With galactic gunge?

SMART SHARK CARS

Smart Shark cars
Are cars with stars on,
Cars with arms on,
And cars with alarms on,
Cars that spark,
And cars that bark,
And cars that you can
See in the dark.
But if you want
A car that starts,
A car that lasts
And won't fall apart,
Don't go to
Smart Shark Cars –
You won't get
Very far!

Which car does Smart Shark drive?

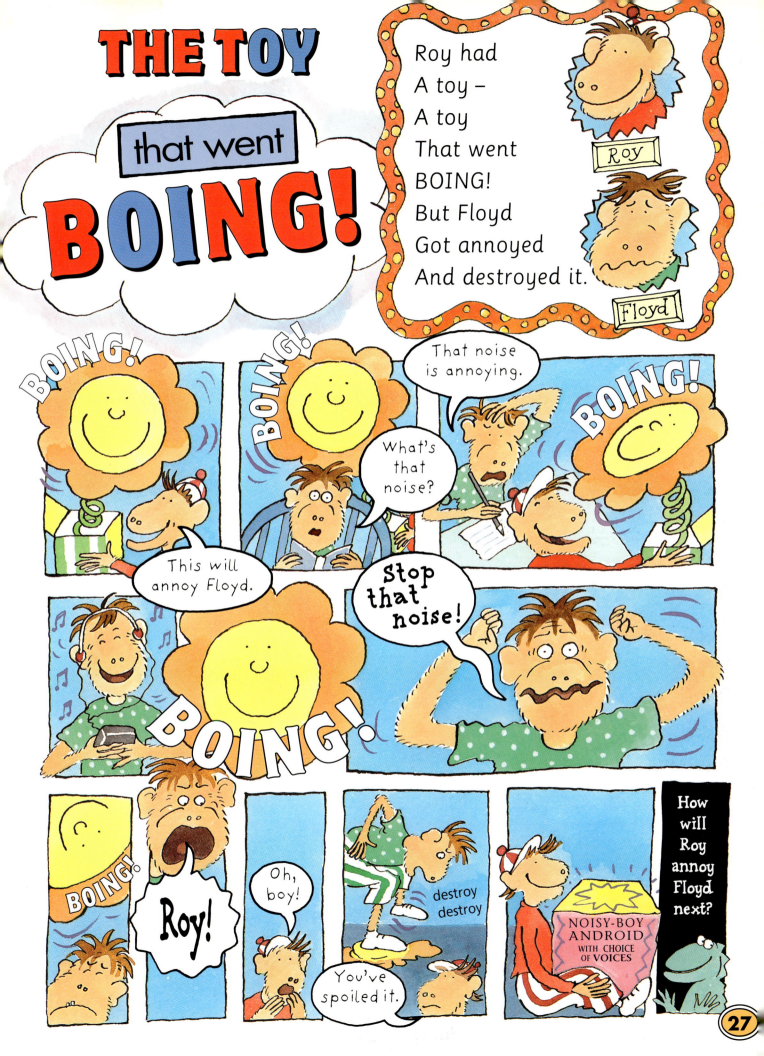

BUSTER BROWN'S HOUSE

Buster Brown,
Buster Brown,
Had the loudest
House in town.
Then Mad Dog Growl
Began to howl.
"HOWL! HOWL!"
Went Mad Dog Growl,
And drowned
The sound
Of Buster Brown.

THE PLACE TO SKATE

Katy Bates
Used to skate
From eight
Till late,
Or even later.
Then she met
An alligator
Who ate her.
Poor Katy Bates!
They saved the skates,
But not the skater.

SHAKES 'N' BAKES

GREEDY SHEEP

Greedy Sheep
Went to sleep
And dreamed.
A greedy dream.
She dreamed
Of a feast
And a greedy beast
Which really
Made her scream!

Mrs G Sheep

1 Greedy Sheep goes to sleep.

peas

3 She eats some peas.

Greedy beast!

green beans

6 The beast eats up the feast.

SCREAM!

9 Greedy Sheep leaps out of bed.

Silly me.

Tea

Coffee

10 It was only a dream!

2 She dreams about a feast.

4 Then a beast sneaks up …

5 and steals a peach.

7 Now the beast needs meat …

8 Greedy Sheep shrieks!

11 The greedy beast wasn't real. Or was he?

I SPY

I spy a pie,
A giant pie.
I spy a bite,
A giant bite.
I spy an eye,
A giant eye –
And the giant eye
Spies me!

1 High in the sky Private Eye spies a pie.

pie

I spy a pie.

A pie in the sky.

A flying pie.

I'm frightened.

It might be a sign.

Let's hide.

4 Private Eye spies the bite.

bite

I spy a giant bite.

What a sight!

The light's too bright.

A giant bite!

5 Then Private Eye gets a fright.

Hi!

I spy a giant eye. Yikes!

eye

2 The pie arrives. It's a giant pie.

3 In the night a giant arrives and takes a bite.

6 But the giant is nice and kind and everyone tries the pie.

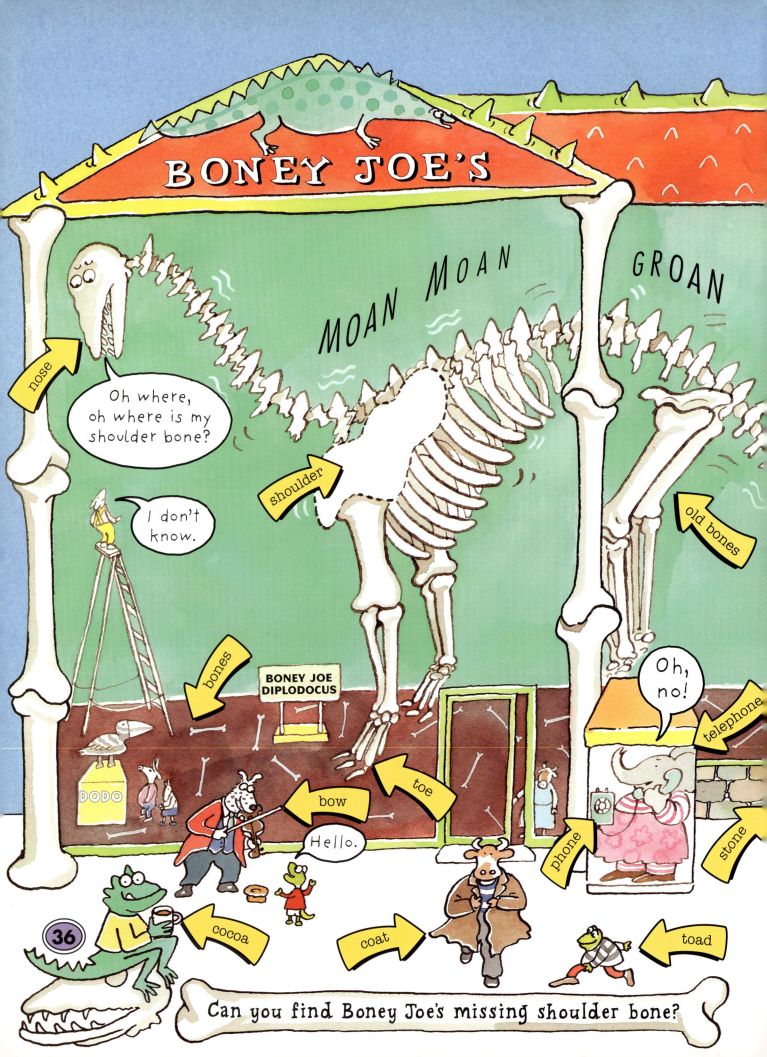

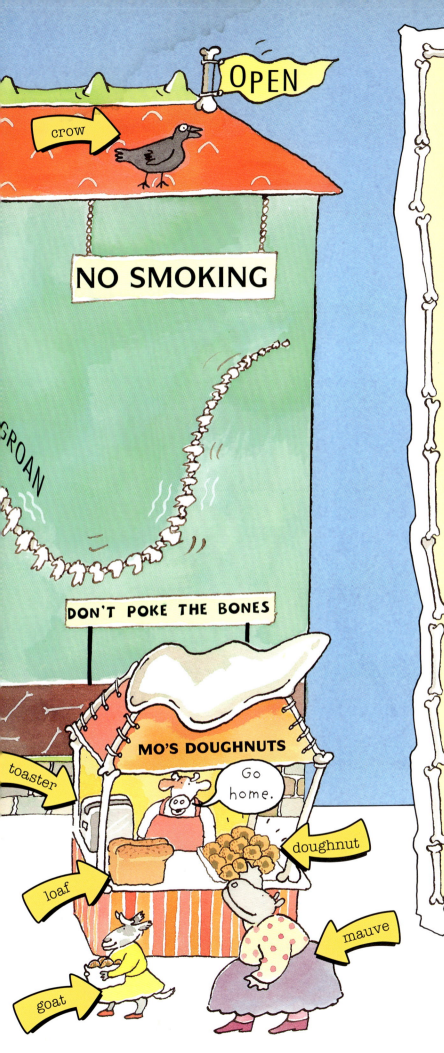

LOADS OF BONES

Don't you know
That Boney Joe
Is only a load of
Cold
Old
Bones!
But if you're alone
With Boney Joe
Those
Cold
Old
Bones
Will moan
And groan,
"Oh where,
Oh where
Is my
Shoulder
Bone?"

GOOD NEWS SALOON

It was noon
In June
At the Good News Saloon,
When a moose
Drinking juice
Put a hoof
Through the roof,
And baboons
Threw spoons
At a snoozing raccoon,
And a newt
In a suit
Tried to shoot
The fruit,
And a stupid
Kangaroo
Put a shoe
In the stew!
Would you
Book a room
At the Good News Saloon?

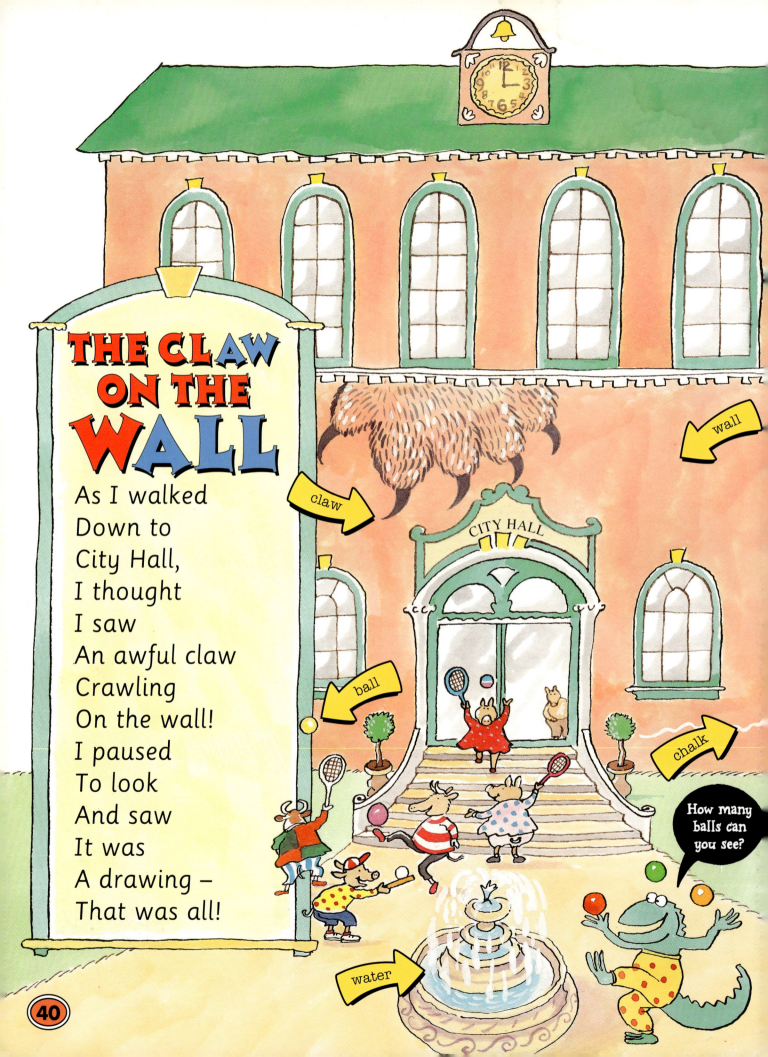

THE CLAW ON THE WALL

As I walked
Down to
City Hall,
I thought
I saw
An awful claw
Crawling
On the wall!
I paused
To look
And saw
It was
A drawing –
That was all!

THE POPCORN STORE

One, two,
Three, four,
Get your popcorn
From the store.
If you drop it
On the floor,
You'll be heading
For the door.

CURLY'S PERFECT PERMS

Who is lurking
Behind the curtain
At Curly's
Perfect Perms?
First, a nurse
About to burst.
Next, a turtle
Turning purple.
Third, a bird
Who looks a nerd,
With the worst perm
In the world!

BEARS AT THE FAIR

A pair of bears
Went to the fair
To take a ride
On the scary chairs.
One didn't dare,
And one didn't care,
And one took a ride
On the scary chairs.
How many bears
Were there?

Doctor Deer's EAR AND HEARING CLINIC

"Dear Doctor Deer,"
Said Mr Steer,
"I fear I've lost
My hearing."
"You'll hear
Quite clear,"
Said Doctor Deer,
"If you
Take off
Your ear-ring!"

MORE WALKER PAPERBACKS
For You to Enjoy

Also by Sarah Hayes

NINE DUCKS NINE

Nine ducks nine walk out in line – and Mr Fox creeps after them.
One by one the ducks make their way down to the rickety bridge, where a big surprise
awaits their foxy pursuer in this amusing cumulative rhyme.

"Simple but entertaining… There is much humour in the watercolour illustrations,
and the book will appeal to all young children." *School Librarian*

0-7445-2018-5　£4.99

THIS IS THE BEAR
illustrated by Helen Craig

Four rollicking cumulative rhymes about the adventures of a boy, a dog and a bear.

"For those ready for their first story, there could be no better choice…
Helen Craig's pictures are just right." *Judy Taylor, The Independent*

0-7445-0969-6　*This Is the Bear*
0-7445-1304-9　*This Is the Bear and the Picnic Lunch*
0-7445-3147-0　*This Is the Bear and the Scary Night*
0-7445-4771-7　*This Is the Bear and the Bad Little Girl*

£4.99 each

THE GRUMPALUMP
illustrated by Barbara Firth

Just what is the grumpalump? A mole can roll on it, a dove can shove it, a yak can whack it and an
armadillo can use it for a pillow. But what is it, and why is it so grumpy?

"Jauntily drawn and painted… Irresistible, easy-to-read fantasy." *The Observer*

0-7445-2021-5　£5.99